RUSSIA

New Freedoms, New Challenges

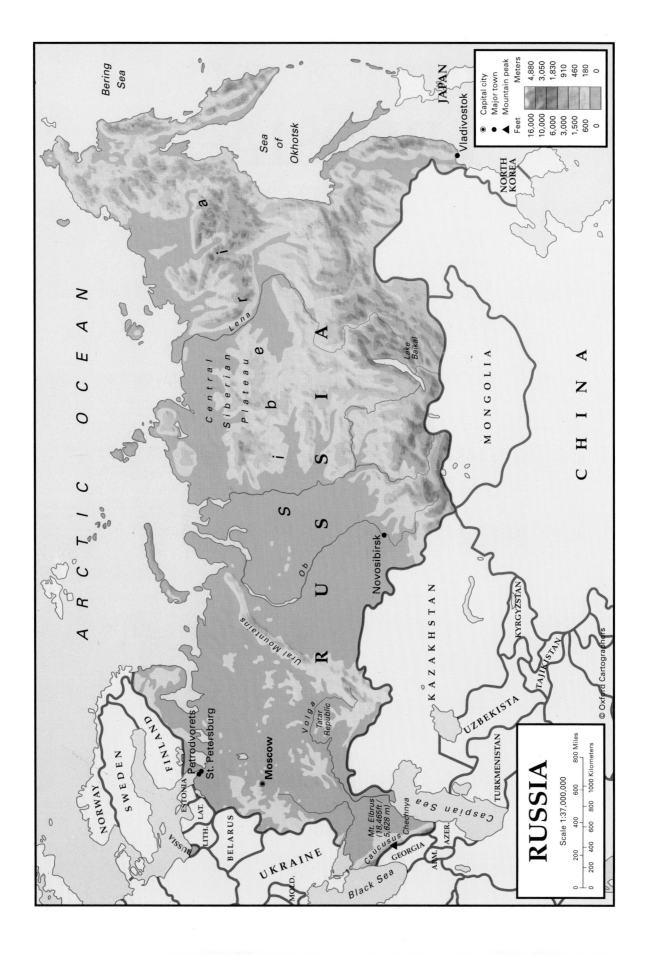

ARCTIC OCEAN

Bering Sea

Sea of Okhotsk

JAPAN

Vladivostok

NORTH KOREA

● Capital city
● Major town
▲ Mountain peak

Meters		Feet
4,880		16,000
3,050		10,000
1,830		6,000
910		3,000
460		1,500
180		600
0		0

S i b e r i a

Central Siberian Plateau

Lena

Lake Baikal

MONGOLIA

CHINA

R U S S I A

Ob

Novosibirsk

KAZAKHSTAN

KYRGYZSTAN

TAJIKISTAN

UZBEKISTA

Ural Mountains

Volga

Tatar Republic

© Oxford Cartographers

NORWAY

SWEDEN

FINLAND

ESTONIA

LITH.

LAT.

RUSSIA

BELARUS

Petrodvorets

St. Petersburg

◉ Moscow

UKRAINE

MOLD.

TURKMENISTAN

Caspian Sea

Chechnya

Caucusus

GEORGIA

ARM.

AZER.

Mt. Elbrus
(18,465ft /
5,628 m)

Black Sea

RUSSIA

Scale 1:37,000,000

0	200	400	600	800 Miles

| 0 | 200 | 400 | 600 | 800 | 1000 Kilometers |

RUSSIA

New Freedoms, New Challenges

Virginia Schomp

BENCHMARK BOOKS

MARSHALL CAVENDISH

NEW YORK

With thanks to Dr. Ronald Meyer of the Harriman Institute (the Russian Institute), Columbia University, New York City, for his gracious assistance and expert advice.

TO MY TWO RICHARDS

Benchmark Books
Marshall Cavendish Corporation
99 White Plains Road
Tarrytown, New York 10591-9001

© Marshall Cavendish Corporation 1996

APR 1996

Library of Congress Cataloging-in-Publication Data

Schomp, Virginia, date.
    Russia—new freedoms, new challenges / by Virginia Schomp.
        p.   cm. — (Exploring cultures of the world)
    Includes bibliographical references.
    ISBN 0-7614-0186-5 (lib. binding)
    1. Russia (Federation)—History—1991– —Juvenile literature.   I. Title.   II. Series.
DK510.76.S36   1996
947.086—dc20   95-15338

SUMMARY: Reviews the geography, history, people, customs, and the arts of Russia.

Printed and bound in Italy

Book design by Carol Matsuyama
Photo research by Laurie Platt Winfrey, Carousel Research, Inc.

Front cover: Yakut women in traditional costume, Siberia
Title page: Moscow youth
Back cover: St. Basil's Cathedral, Moscow

Photo Credits

Front and back covers: courtesy of SOVFOTO/EASTFOTO; title page: courtesy of Bill Bachmann/Photo Researchers; page 6:Archiv/Photo Researchers; page 10: A. Nechayev/ SOVFOTO/EASTFOTO;page 13:John O'Hagan/Photo Researchers; pages 15, 22, 24, 38, 39, 40 (*top*),45, 47, 56:SOVFOTO/EASTFOTO; page 16:Wernher Collection, Suton Hoo/Laurie Platt Winfrey, Carousel Research; page 18: Anne S. K. Brown Military Collection/Laurie Platt Winfrey, Carousel Research; page 20: SOVFOTO; page 27: Alexandra Avakian/ Woodfin Camp; pages 28, 31(*top*), 40 (*middle*), 52 (*top*): Jeff Greenberg/Photo Researchers; page 31 (*bottom*):Chuck Nacke/Woodfin Camp; pages 32, 34, 36, 48: Sylvain Grandadam/ Photo Researchers; page 40 (*bottom*): Hannale Rantala /Woodfin Camp; page 43: Bill Bachmann/Photo Researchers; page 52 (*bottom*): James Wilson/Woodfin Camp; page 54: Bob Saler/Photo Researchers; page 55: George Holten/Photo Researchers

Contents

Peter the Great, ruler of Russia from 1682 to 1725, transformed his backward nation into a great Western power.

1
GEOGRAPHY AND HISTORY

Russia Then and Now

Czar Peter's Progress

*I*n the spring of 1697 a splendid parade of carts, horses, and riders rolled noisily across Russia's western border. Among the hundreds of bearded soldiers, richly robed nobles, drummers, and trumpeters rode a roughly dressed sailor called Peter Mikhailov. The name and the clothes were a disguise. The tall, shy young man was really Czar Peter I, supreme ruler of all Russia.

No czar had ever left Russia before, except to make war. But Peter had a mission. He was determined to raise his people from the ignorance that kept them poor and isolated. He believed that his giant nation could become a great world power. But first he must learn what made other nations great.

For eighteen months the Russian procession traveled across Western Europe. The czar's presence was supposed to be a secret, but at six feet seven inches, Peter tended to stand out from the crowd. Another clue to his identity was the mysterious illness that made the left side of his face twitch uncontrollably. Still, Europe's governors and kings respected Peter's wish for privacy. Treating his noblemen to long, boring ceremonies in honor of Russia's czar, they left the czar himself free to explore.

In Sweden Peter studied the art of modern fortress making, sketching and measuring every inch of the mighty stone Riga Fortress. His Swedish hosts watched politely but nervously—Riga had been built just forty years earlier for defense against Russia's armies.

In Holland Peter worked as a carpenter to learn shipbuilding. Reporting each morning with his tools slung over his back, "Master Peter" helped put together every nail and timber of a new square-sailed warship. The czar completed his study of modern ship design and workmanship in England, home of the world's most powerful navy.

Peter also visited museums, factories, workshops, churches, and laboratories. He "discovered" ice skates, wheelbarrows, wind dials, stuffed crocodiles, and the amazing new microscope. Driven always not only to see but to understand, he studied under the West's finest scientists, engineers, printers, and doctors. Peter even became so handy at pulling teeth that he took to carrying around a set of dentist's tools . . . and his companions took to hiding their toothaches.

When at last Peter returned to Russia, crowds of court officials ran to welcome him. The czar pulled out a pair of scissors and began snipping off the astonished men's beards. To Peter, long beards were a sign of Russia's past; the time had come for a new day. That glorious new beginning saw an end to many worn-out customs. In their place Peter introduced the advancements of the Western world. Today he is known as the founder of modern Russia. In his time he was honored as Peter the Great.

A Vast and Varied Land

The Two Russias

The borders of Peter the Great's mighty empire have shifted a few miles, but Russia is still a giant. From the icy Arctic Ocean it stretches south to the Black Sea; from the rolling plains of Eastern Europe it sprawls east to the Pacific Ocean. Its lands cover much of two continents—Europe and Asia—and more than one-sixth of the world's land surface. That makes Russia the largest country on earth.

Within its far-flung borders, Russia divides into two regions—west and east. The western one-third of the country is home to 80 percent of the people. It contains all of Russia's largest cities, 85 percent of its business and manufacturing, and 90 percent of its productive farmland. But because this region is so heavily populated and developed, many of its natural resources—lumber, coal, iron ore—are running out.

Natural resources overflow in eastern Russia. This vast region, known as Siberia, holds miles of green forests and rich deposits of oil, coal, natural gas, uranium, diamonds, and gold. But most of the riches remain locked beneath the land. Siberia is one of the coldest places on earth, and few people can stand to live and work in its harsh wilderness.

Fertile Plains, Frozen Tundra

From frozen wastes to soaring mountaintops, Russia has nearly every type of land feature. Most of western Russia is one enormous plain, with miles of flat land and gently rolling hills. At the eastern edge of the plain rise the Ural Mountains. This long, low mountain chain, which slices through Russia from top to bottom, is usually considered the dividing line between Europe and Asia. East of the Urals, in Siberia, is another vast plain, surrounded by a wilderness of steplike plateaus, high mountains, and deep valleys.

Covering Russia's plains and plateaus, mountains and valleys, are five different types of environments. The northernmost environmental layer is Arctic desert, ice-covered and nearly lifeless. South of this stretches the tundra, a cold, tree-

A hot spring in the midst of frozen Siberia shows the colorful contrasts of Russia's countryside.

less plain where winters are long, the ground is frozen almost all year, and little grows except grass and moss. South of the tundra is a great layer of forestland called the taiga (TY-ga), which covers nearly half of Russia. Below the taiga are the steppes—grassy meadows that hold the country's richest soil and best farmland. And south of the steppes, along the eastern shores of the Caspian Sea, are small sections of desert.

Winding Waterways

Crisscrossing this varied landscape is a maze of rivers great and small. Russia has more than 100,000 waterways, including five of the longest rivers in the world. Chief among these is the Volga. The longest river in Europe, "Mother Volga" winds more than two thousand miles on its journey south from the Valdai Hills in northwest Russia. Along the way, its waters carry cargo and passengers, irrigate farmland, provide electricity through water-powered electric plants, and offer rich fishing and a cool dip beside sandy beaches.

The Volga's final stop is the Caspian Sea, on Russia's southern border. This "sea" is really the world's largest saltwater lake. The largest freshwater lake in the world is Lake Baikal (by-KAHL), in Siberia. If the 5,315-foot (1,620 meters)-deep Lake Baikal was emptied, it would take all the rivers in the world nearly a year to fill it again.

Cold, Colder . . . Hot?

Russian winters are long and bitter cold. Moscow, in northwest Russia, is covered in snow five months a year, and winter temperatures average 18°F (-7.7°C). Even that must look appealing from northeast Siberia. Ice and snow blanket that chilly region eight to nine months a year, and January often brings temperatures below -50°F (-45°C).

The surprise is that Russia's short summers also go to extremes. July in Moscow can send temperatures soaring into the 70s or 80s (22–30°C), and during northeast Siberia's two-month heat wave, temperatures can hit 100°F (38°C).

Splendid Cities

Russia's capital, Moscow, offers something for everyone. The third largest city in the world, Moscow has fascinating historical sights, magnificent architecture, and cultural attractions from fine ballet to rock-and-roll concerts. Nearly nine million people live in this great center of culture, politics, and industry.

Four hundred miles north of Moscow lies Russia's second largest city, St. Petersburg. Beautiful St. Petersburg was founded by Peter the Great as a "window to the West." Its dazzling palaces, mansions, bridges, and fountains serve as lasting reminders of Peter's plan to make Russia a showplace of Western culture.

Russia through the Ages

The Rise of Rus

Mighty Moscow was once a wooden fort on a hill, St. Petersburg a mosquito-filled swamp. And centuries ago Russia itself was a vast wilderness dotted with simple farming villages.

The farmers were Slavs, an ancient people who settled in the rich forests of the taiga around A.D. 300. By the eighth century, Slavic tribes had built up lively trading cities all along the Volga River. Then, wandering bands of warrior-adventurers called Varangians thundered down from Scandinavia. When a band called the Varangian Russes conquered important Slavic trading centers, the region became known as the Land of Rus.

Rus grew to become a large and powerful state. But the thirteenth century brought new conquerors. Armies of Mongols—brutal warriors from eastern Asia—swept like wildfire through the Russian cities. By 1240 all of Rus had been swallowed up in the Mongolian empire.

The Mongols ruled for 250 years. All that time Rus was cut

St. Basil's Cathedral, the jewel of Moscow, is known around the world as a symbol of Russia's might and majesty.

off from the rest of the world. Then, in 1480, Ivan the Great, prince of the Russian city Moscow, refused to pay the Mongols' taxes. A Mongol army set out with armor clanking, but turned back at the sight of Moscow's determined forces. That quiet retreat marked the end of Mongol rule.

Under the Czars

Free Russia took Moscow as its capital and Ivan the Great as its leader. Fifty years later his grandson Ivan IV became prince of Moscow. The young Ivan named himself czar, from the Russian word for *caesar,* or emperor. His conquests pushed Russia's borders north, east, and south. But the first czar was also a madman whose delight in torture and murder earned him the name Ivan the Terrible.

A long line of czars followed Ivan, ruling Russia for the next three centuries. The czars had absolute, unlimited power—their word was law. Beneath the czars were wealthy nobles and soldiers, who owned most of the land. At the bottom of the ladder were the serfs, poor laborers who were bought and sold like animals.

Under the czars, Russia grew in size and influence. It became a major European power under Peter the Great. Half a century later Empress Catherine the Great built it into one of the largest empires in the world. In 1812 the Russian giant proved its might by defeating the invading forces of French emperor Napoleon Bonaparte.

The Russian Revolution

Czar Alexander II freed the serfs in 1861. But as Russia entered the twentieth century, the former serfs were still desperately poor and had no political rights. Peasants and factory workers

Czar Ivan the Terrible laid the foundations for a mighty empire but was a cruel and murderous ruler.

Catherine the Great, empress from 1762 to 1796, was a strong ruler who fulfilled Peter the Great's dream of making Russia one of the world's greatest empires.

began to demonstrate for equality. Though they were often answered with rifle fire, the demonstrations continued.

In 1914 Russia entered World War I, siding with Britain and France against the expanding German empire. Russia was unprepared for war. Its cities suffered shortages of food and fuel. By March 1917 the Russian people were starving. Riots broke out, and soldiers were called in to restore order. They joined the rioters instead. On March 15 the last czar of Russia, Nicholas II, was forced to give up the throne.

Communist Rule

Months of disorder followed the end of czarist rule. Into the confusion stepped Vladimir Lenin, leader of a group of revolutionaries who believed in communism—the system in which all goods are owned and controlled by the government. Lenin and the Communists seized control of nearly all the lands of the old Russian Empire. In 1922 they divided the empire into a number of smaller republics. They named their new country the Union of Soviet Socialist Republics, or Soviet Union.

Lenin's government took over private lands and businesses. After Lenin's death, the dictator Joseph Stalin carried these "reforms" further. Stalin's government told farms and factories what to produce, and distributed food and other goods among the Soviet people. But the system didn't work. In the 1930s millions of people died in a nationwide famine. Millions more were imprisoned or killed for criticizing the Communists' programs.

The Soviet Union was invaded in 1941 by the forces of Adolf Hitler, the German dictator who had started World War II. By the time the war ended in 1945, more than 25 million Soviet people had died. After the war Soviet leaders built their

Soldiers carry a portrait of Russia's last czar, Nicholas II, to the fire during the Russian Revolution.

nation into an industrial giant and great world power. But the Soviet economy and way of life continued to crumble. Store shelves stood empty. Finding milk, bread, and other basic goods was a daily struggle. Just as hard on the Soviet people were the Communist controls on work, speech, travel, housing, and nearly every other part of life.

THE SOVIET REPUBLICS

The Union of Soviet Socialist Republics, also called the Soviet Union or the USSR, included most of the lands of the old Russian Empire. It was made up of fifteen republics, of which Russia was by far the largest. In fact, because of the Russian Republic's size and its role as center of the Soviet government, the name Russia often was used to refer to the whole USSR.

The fifteen Soviet republics—all independent nations today—included:

Armenia*	Georgia	Lithuania	Turkmenistan
Azerbaijan*	Kazakhstan*	Moldova*	Ukraine*
Belarus*	Kyrgyzstan*	Russia*	Uzbekistan*
Estonia	Latvia	Tajikistan*	

*These former republics are now members of the Commonwealth of Independent States.

The Journey to Freedom

In 1985 Mikhail Gorbachev (mi-KALE gor-ba-CHAHV) became leader of the Soviet Union. Gorbachev loosened controls on farms and factories and allowed the first free elections. But his reforms frightened top Communist officials. In August 1991 they plotted to overthrow Gorbachev. The people of Moscow filled the streets, demanding the right to choose their own leaders. The plotters themselves were overthrown, and Gorbachev shut down the Communist Party. One by one the Soviet republics declared independence. By December Soviet leader Gorbachev had resigned. The Soviet Union no longer existed.

The leader of the opposition to the Communist plotters was Boris Yeltsin, the newly elected president of the Russian Republic. Yeltsin and the leaders of ten other former Soviet re-

Soldiers and crowds fill the streets in front of the Russian parliament building during the 1991 coup.

publics agreed to form the Commonwealth of Independent States, or CIS. The CIS is not a country but a union of independent nations that have agreed to help each other in the struggle to build successful new democracies.

The task has not been easy. Under the Communists, the central government controlled all farms, factories, and businesses and set the price at which all goods were sold. Russians today are free to run their own businesses and charge whatever they choose. Under the new system, prices have soared. A loaf of bread that used to cost a few pennies now costs several dollars. Most families have barely enough money for food and nothing left over for other goods.

These hardships have led some Russians to call for a return to communism. Others tighten their belts and point with pride to their new freedoms. It is too early to tell which side will win out. But with the strength and patience of a people who have survived many bitter winters, Russia may yet take its place among the world's great democracies.

RUSSIAN GOVERNMENT

Russia is a democratic republic. The governing body is called the Federal Assembly. It has two houses: the upper Council of the Federation, which has two representatives from each region, and the lower State Duma with 450 members.

Russia's new constitution, approved in 1993, makes the president head of state and the prime minister, who is appointed by the president, head of government. The president serves for four years and has broad powers, while those of the prime minister are limited.

The highest court in the land is the Constitutional Court. Established in 1992, it rules on the constitutionality of the country's laws. The president is responsible for appointing its twenty-one members.

The cobblestoned streets of Red Square are a favorite spot for strollers on a rainy evening in Moscow.

2
THE PEOPLE

Meet the Russians

Generous, friendly, helpful, curious—these are the qualities that visitors to Russia first notice in the people. Russians enjoy sharing food and gifts with friends and with strangers. A visitor to even a poor Russian home is likely to be treated to a feast. And along with the outpouring of food and drink, Russian hosts always treat foreign guests to a flood of questions about the outside world.

Behind their warm and openhearted manners, Russians also have a solemn side that some call the "Russian soul." A long history of hardship has taught the people not to expect too much. While the very young may have bright hopes for the future, most older Russians shrug off talk of better days. "Life has always been a struggle," they say with patience and a grim smile. "Will tomorrow be any different? Let's wait and see."

Many Cultures . . .

Russians love their country and are proud of its important place in world history. They also take pride in their individual cultures. For the citizens of Russia are not all of Russian ancestry. Out of the country's more than 149 million people, about 82 percent are ethnic Russians, descended from the Slavs who lived in the state of Rus. The other 18 percent, or about 27 million people, belong to about 120 different ethnic groups.

These nationalities include Tatars, Ukrainians, Belarussians, Chuvashes, and many others. The Tatars descended from the Mongols who invaded thirteenth-century Russia. The ancestors of the Ukrainians and Belarussians came from nearby Ukraine and Belarus. The Chuvashes trace their roots to an ancient people of central Asia. Many of Russia's ethnic groups live in self-governing territories called autonomous republics.

The Communists treated Russia's smaller ethnic groups worse than the Russian majority. But today all citizens have

Life is a blend of traditional and modern influences for the people of Yakut, an autonomous republic in northeast Siberia.

the same rights and privileges. Relations between Russia and its minority groups are not always easy, though. In December 1994, President Yeltsin sent troops to the region of Chechnya. The people there wanted complete independence from Russia. Many deaths and injuries have occurred on both sides as a result of the warfare.

. . . Many Tongues

Along with their special ancestry and customs, Russia's different ethnic groups have their own languages. Tatars speak Tatar. Chuvashes speak Chuvash. But all groups speak the country's official language, Russian, too.

Russian is a Slavic language, quite different from English both in how it sounds and how it looks. Rich, musical, and complex, it is a difficult language for English-speaking people to learn. Russian is written in Cyrillic (seh-RI-lik), an alphabet of thirty-three letters, most of which are unlike any letter in the Roman (English) alphabet. The Russian word for *hello* would be written this way:

Здравствуйте

It would sound like this: zdrahst-VOO-yeh-teh.

City Life, Country Life

About three-quarters of Russia's people live elbow to elbow in the cities. Nearly all Russian cities are overcrowded. Moscow alone holds nearly nine million people—that's the total population of the American states of Washington, Arkansas, and New Hampshire combined.

Not surprisingly, finding housing for so many people is a problem. Most city families live in tiny apartments in blocks of

SAY IT IN RUSSIAN

Here is how you would say some common words and phrases in Russian.

hello	zdrahst-VOO-yeh-teh (or, less formally, pri-VET)
good-bye	da-svee-DAHN-yah
My name is ...	men-YAH ZAH-voot
How are you?	KAHK dee-LAH?
please	poh-ZHAH-loo-stah
thank you	spah-SEE-bah
excuse me	eez-vee-NEET-yeh
I understand	YAH pah-nee-MAH-yoo
yes	dah
no	nyet
mother	MAH-mah
father	PAH-pah
sister	syeh-STRAH
brother	braht
grandmother	BAH-boosh-keh
grandfather	DYEH-doosh-key

high-rise buildings. Often children, parents, and grandparents all live together, or two families share an apartment. With just two bedrooms, a small living/eating area, and a tiny kitchen and bathroom, a Russian two-family apartment doesn't allow much space for relaxing or playing.

Outside, the city streets are jammed with people on foot, bicycles, and buses. Very few Russians can afford their own car, but getting to work or school is easy on the public buses and subways. An everyday sight on city streets are long lines of patient shoppers waiting for a shipment of sugar or fresh cheese. From sidewalk booths, or kiosks, vendors sell fruit or vegetables from their gardens, homemade rugs, used shoes, and other valuables.

Most of the people of Russia's countryside live in large

Shoppers jam the corridors of GUM, Moscow's biggest department store.

villages and share the work on a nearby farm. Their homes are small wooden houses, frequently without electricity, running water, or indoor toilets. The people get around by foot, bicycle, or horse and sleigh. Country roads often are unpaved, and in the spring and fall, rain or melting snow turn them into rivers of mud.

Country life is hard in other ways, too. The schools are not as good as in the cities, and there may not be a doctor for many miles. Summers are short and filled with planting and harvesting; winters are long, cold, and dull. On winter evenings, while the elders talk and smoke their pipes, young people often sit dreaming of moving to the bustling cities someday.

Modern Russian teenagers live and dress much like young people in the United States.

INSIDE RUSSIAN NAMES

Russian names tell a lot about a person. From the middle name we know what the person's father was called, and from the last name we can tell whether someone is a man or a woman.

Most people have three names. The first is their *given* name. Parents usually call their children by a nickname based on their given name. Elena is called Lena. Mikhail's nickname is Misha.

The second name is the *patronymic* (pa-treh-NI-mik)—the father's first name plus an ending. Elena Ivanovna is the daughter of Ivan. Mikhail Vladimirovich is the son of Vladimir.

The last name is the *family* name. Women and girls add an *a* to their last name. So Elena Ivanovna Surikov*a* would have to be a girl, and her brother's last name would be Surikov.

The Changing Workplace

In the Soviet Union everyone had a job. But pay was low, and it was set by the government. Hard work was not rewarded with higher pay; in fact, the best workers often were punished for sticking out from the crowd. Across Russia the workers' sarcastic saying became "You pretend to pay me and I'll pretend to work."

The new Russia's leaders want to return all farms and businesses to private owners. They are trying to replace the government-controlled system with a market economy, where businesses can set their own wages and prices, and profit from the goods they produce. They believe the Western-style market economy will be more efficient and productive than the old Soviet system. But trying to change the way the largest country in the world operates has turned the Russian workplace upside down.

Many Russian factory workers have found themselves out of a job for the first time in their lives. Under Soviet managers, factories did not keep up to date with modern production methods. Now many factories have been forced to close because they cannot compete with foreign companies making better goods at lower prices.

Old-fashioned equipment also has made mining in Russia slow, inefficient, and dangerous. The harsh climate in Siberia, where most of Russia's minerals and fuels lie under frozen ground, adds to the difficulty of mining the country's resources. Today Russia's leaders are looking for money and know-how from other nations to help make their factories and mines modern and productive.

Forestry, fishing, and farming are also important occupations in Russia. Vast forests of evergreens and birch trees put many thousands of Russians to work in sawmills and paper plants. In the fertile fishing grounds of the nation's coastal waters, rivers, and lakes, fishermen net cod, haddock, herring, sturgeon, and salmon. On Russia's farms workers produce abundant crops of wheat, barley, rye, oats, potatoes, and sugar beets. But in spite of Russia's bountiful waters and fields, city store shelves are never full, because food often spoils before reaching the market.

Russia's leaders are working to build a better system for transporting cut trees, fish, and farm products. They also are encouraging farmworkers to set up their own independent operations. In the Soviet Union people had to work together on huge government-owned collective farms. Most still share the work on large community farms, because they cannot afford the land and tools needed to strike out on their own.

One of the most exciting changes in the Russian workplace has been the growth of small, private businesses. Under the Communists, it was illegal to own a business. Now many Russians are opening their own small restaurants, barber-

Despite changes and hardships in the new Russia, work goes on at many farms and factories.

shops, dry cleaners, clothing stores, and advertising agencies. A new word has entered the Russian language to describe these independent merchants: *biznesmeni*.

The struggle to build a new democratic nation has brought much change and hardship to Russia's workers. But the people hope to use their country's rich natural resources to make life easier. Perhaps the most valuable of these riches are the patience, pride, and generosity of the great-hearted Russian people.

The table is set for a festival meal in this St. Petersburg family home.

3
FAMILY LIFE, FESTIVALS, AND FOOD

Reviving Faith and Festivals

At Home with the Russians

In Russia the family is the center of life, and children are the center of the family. Most city families can only afford to have one child. That child, warmly loved and pampered, is the parents' special joy and their symbol of hope for the future.

Families in the countryside often are larger than city families, but there, too, children are cherished. And whether the basic family includes one child or many, nearly all Russians also have a large and close extended family. On city streets it is common to see entire families—parents, children, aunts, uncles, cousins, and grandparents—enjoying the parks, museums, and public gardens together.

Grown children usually live with their parents for many years after they marry and have children of their own. The family's grandmother, or babushka (BAH-boosh-keh), plays a very important role in the home and in Russian society. It is the babushka who helps care for the children, cooks, shops, sews, and cleans. To help the family out by earning a few extra coins, sixty- and seventy-year-old babushkas often take part-time jobs shoveling snow and washing floors.

Six hardworking babushkas, or "grandmothers," take a break from their busy routines.

All these contributions make the life of the young Russian mother a bit easier, but it is still a busy life indeed. Most Russian women have full-time jobs and at the same time are responsible for all the household work and child care. In Russia the father is king of the family, and the king doesn't change diapers. Women take care of the children and do the grocery shopping, cooking, and cleaning. After a hard week of work, women must hand-wash the family's clothes, hang them out to dry, scrub the floors, and beat the dust from rugs draped over clotheslines.

The Rebirth of Religion

Just as they have always helped keep families together, babushkas have helped the Russian people hold on to their religious faith. The Communists closed many churches and seized church property. Schoolchildren were taught that religion was bad, and many workers who expressed religious beliefs lost good jobs, homes, or other privileges. Through all this, handfuls of kerchiefed babushkas still went to church each day, lit candles in memory of loved ones, and found priests to secretly baptize their grandchildren.

After the fall of communism churches began to reopen. Russia today is experiencing a religious revival, with churches packed on Sundays and tens of thousands of adults being baptized. Elderly women and men still make up the majority of worshipers. But growing numbers of young people are overcoming a lifetime of antireligious training to return to the centuries-old faith of their people.

The Russian Orthodox Church is by far the country's largest and most deeply rooted faith. Unchanged through the ages, the Orthodox Church service is a stirring pageant of rich and solemn ceremony. Worshipers stand for hours as bearded priests in princely robes chant holy words through mists of smoky incense and dim candlelight.

Other, smaller Christian groups in Russia include Baptists, Roman Catholics, Lutherans, and Evangelists. In Moscow and many southern regions, Muslims practice Islam, a religion that began in the Middle East, in which the people worship one god, called Allah. There also are approximately

After decades in which the Communists tried to stamp out religion, Russians of all ages are rediscovering their faith.

two million Russian Jews. In Russia, Jews are considered an ethnic rather than a religious group, and only about 10 percent of the Jews actively practice their faith.

Holy Days and Holidays

Along with the revival of religion in Russia has come the rebirth of religious holidays. Christmas is the children's favorite. Celebrated on January 7, it follows the three-week-long Winter Festival. Decorated fir trees brighten homes, cities hold special sports events, carnivals, and circuses, and children eagerly watch for the jolly man in the red suit whom they call Grandfather Frost.

Easter is another joyous religious celebration. Children stay up late for midnight church service, then enjoy special Easter cakes and cookies. *Pysanky* (pi-SAHN-kee)—beautiful eggs painted with wax and bright dyes—are prized Easter gifts.

The Russians' most popular nonreligious holiday is New Year's Day, on January 1, a time for gifts and parties. May 1 is Spring Day, also known as May Day, a holiday celebrated with parades and family get-togethers. Women's hard work is honored on Women's Day, March 8, and the end of World War II is remembered on May 9, Victory Day. On August 21, schools and businesses close to mark the day the Communist plot to overthrow Mikhail Gorbachev collapsed and a new democratic Russia was born.

Creative Cookery

Holiday meals call for special food treats. Koulich is a white Easter cake packed with raisins, nuts, and candied fruit. Caviar, especially black caviar made from the eggs of the Caspian Sea's Beluga sturgeon, is an expensive but beloved holiday treat.

For everyday meals, though, the Russian diet is not very exciting. Food shortages and high prices force most Russians to live mainly on bread, pasta, and potatoes. Carrots, onions, beets, and cabbage usually are easy to find, too. People who own a small summer house, or dacha (DAH-cheh), gather wild mushrooms and grow and can their own vegetables. Otherwise, most Russians generally do without fresh green vegetables, fruits, and meat.

Even with such limited ingredients, the inventive Russian cook creates many hearty dishes. Borscht is a popular soup made from beets, served hot or cold with a spoonful of sour cream. Blini are thin pancakes rolled around salted fish or other fillings. Piroshki (peh-rawsh-KEE), baked or fried dumplings, can be filled with cabbage or meat for the main meal or with jam or fruit for dessert. Kulibiaka, small baked or fried pies, are

Students at a cooking school in Moscow proudly show a tray of piroshki just out of the oven.

stuffed with layers of cabbage, potatoes, mushrooms, chicken, or other vegetables and meats. Even the simple potato can be transformed into a variety of dishes, including pancakes, dumplings, and a baked pudding called potato kugel.

With their meals both adults and children drink milk, soda, seltzer water, or hot tea. Adults also enjoy kvass, a cold drink like beer, made from black bread and honey. And most adults, especially men, also drink plenty of vodka, a strong alcoholic beverage.

BIG MAC IN MOSCOW

In Soviet restaurants the meals were unappetizing, tables were dirty, and customers had to drag lead-footed waiters out of the kitchen. So in 1990, when the first McDonald's opened in Moscow, Russians lined up for blocks to get a taste of Western-style food and service.

Today the low value of the Russian dollar, the ruble, means that buying a Big Mac could cost a Russian worker a whole week's pay. But still, Russians come by the tens of thousands to McDonald's and its Moscow neighbors Pizza Hut and Baskin-Robbins. They admire the sparkling-clean tables, floors, and bathrooms, and marvel at the smiling Russians who serve the food. They sample the exotic *gambourgers* and other Western-style treats. And they don't even grumble when enjoying "fast food" means standing in line for hours.

Staff members celebrate the opening of Moscow's second McDonald's.

Exercise for the mind, body, and spirit are all part of the Russian school day.

4
SCHOOL AND RECREATION

In the Classroom and Out

Education got top marks in the Soviet Union. The Soviets' goal of making the country an industrial giant depended on well-trained, well-educated workers. To reach their goal, they made education free, and they required that all children go to school. Because of their programs nearly every Russian citizen is able to read and write.

But Soviet education was as strictly controlled as every other government program. Students spent much time learning about communism's benefits and the evils of democracy and of privately owned businesses. History lessons were built on lies designed to make the Soviet Union the hero of every world event. Learning meant memorizing, and there was no room for discussion or independent thought.

The end of communism breathed new life into this rigid system. Today Russian textbooks are being rewritten to remove falsehoods. New classes are being taught in world literature, religion, history, and modern economics. Many teachers are beginning to encourage their students' curiosity. They are talking *with* students, not *at* them, and designing classwork that lets young people think for themselves instead of just memorizing facts.

Education is still very important in Russia—perhaps more important than ever. For Russians know that solving their country's problems and building a strong new democracy will take all the knowledge and creative thinking of today's young students.

The Educational Ladder

Russian children begin school at age seven, and they must attend for at least nine years. They go to primary school for grades one through four and middle school for grades five through nine. If they continue on—and a little over half of Russia's students do—grades ten and eleven are spent in high school. In Russia going to high school means attending either a secondary school or a vocational school.

In primary and middle school, major subjects include science, mathematics, reading, writing, physical fitness, and social studies. When students finish middle school, they take a national exam. If they do well, they may choose to enroll in secondary school. There they will concentrate on one course of study, which might be science, math, languages, literature, social studies, or sports. If their scores on the exam are low, they can attend vocational school, where they will be trained for work in a trade, such as auto mechanics.

Less than a quarter of Russian students go on from high school to higher education. Students must score high grades on a tough entrance exam to be admitted to a university, medical school, or scientific institute. There are more than five hundred institutes of higher learning in Russia, and it takes five years to earn a degree in a science or profession.

Let's Go to School

Imagine you are a student in a Russian school. You have to be prepared to work hard. You go to school six days a week. You have lots of homework, at least one or two hours a night. And you begin learning complicated science and math as early as first grade.

The school day starts at eight o'clock. Don't be late—the

Creative self-expression was frowned on by the Soviet Communists but is encouraged in Russia's schools today.

teacher is strict! You sit at a wooden desk in a crowded classroom. Your school building is old and needs repairs, but you still feel lucky—many Russian schools have no heat, running water, or indoor toilets. Besides, your classroom is cozy and cheerful. The walls are covered with painted scenes from Russian folktales, lace curtains line the windows, and the teacher's desk is always bright with flowers.

The day begins with reading and writing. You work in Russian, but children from minority groups in many regions are taught in their own native language. Twice a week you study English, too. All Russian schoolchildren learn a foreign language.

After reading and writing comes math. The teacher calls you to the chalkboard to solve a problem in algebra. You're nervous, but you get the answer right. Then comes lunch. It's your turn to serve. You clean and set the lunchroom table, then give each of your classmates a small bowl of fish soup, a potato pancake, and a chunk of bread.

After lunch you have physical fitness. Today it's gymnastics; tomorrow you might play volleyball or soccer. The school has no history books, so for the history lesson this afternoon your teacher has brought a magazine article about Russia's role in World War II. She reads it, and you take notes. Afterward the class talks about the war. Everyone is eager for a turn; when the Communists were in power, the teacher was the only one who got to talk in class. Then comes a science exam. You check your answers twice and hope to get the best grade, 5. You wouldn't dare bring home a 1!

School ends at two o'clock, but you stick around for soccer practice. Then it's home for supper, much too much homework, and an early lights-out.

School's Out

In their free time, Russians enjoy reading, watching television, and going to museums, plays, concerts, and movies. Only big cities have movie houses, but in the country, people can watch movies at the local "palace of culture," or community recreation center.

Sports are also very popular in Russia. There are countless athletic clubs, recreation centers, stadiums, sports camps, and other facilities for playing and watching sporting events. Some of the world's best athletes have come from Russia, and the country's champions have broken many Olympic and world records.

Young—but very serious—soccer players battle it out on court.

Russia's number-one sport is soccer. Other favorites include gymnastics, basketball, volleyball, track-and-field, weight lifting, and wrestling. American-style baseball is a new and growing pastime in Russia, but children have long played a similar game called *lapta*. Russian children also play a down-sized version of soccer, and practice self-defense with a style of wrestling and judo called sambo.

In the winter, ice hockey, ice skating, and cross-country skiing are popular. Children also enjoy playing in the snow. They build snow people and paint makeup on their snow women's faces.

To exercise the mind, both children and adults like to play chess. Training for chess begins in first grade, and by fifth grade, students are learning the winning plays of chess champions. Many Russians are famous for capturing the world chess championship. And would-be champions flock to Russia's parks even on winter days to play chess in the open air.

Vacation Time

Russian schools are closed in July and August, so the summer is when most families take a vacation. Trips to the sea, the mountains, and the big cities are popular. Families swim, boat, and fish in the Black Sea or Baltic Sea, hike in the Caucasus Mountains, or visit the cities' museums, circuses, and puppet shows. Today, though, high prices have made these traditional vacation trips too expensive for many people.

Fortunately there is still an inexpensive way for many families to have summer fun. More than half of the Russian people own country cottages, or dachas, where they spend summer vacations and occasional weekends. Most dachas are little more than small wooden shacks, often without heat or

46

running water. But there usually is a river nearby for swimming and fishing, and a small plot of land for growing fruits and vegetables. And there is fresh air and sunshine, and wide-open spaces for people tired of life in the crowded cities.

GOOD CLEAN FUN

You may not think of bathing as the best way to have fun. But in Russia public bathhouses are more than just a place to get clean. People go to the baths to relax with friends in a room filled with superheated steam. Men and women have their own separate bathhouses, and the entrance fee is just a few pennies. For a little bit more, you can even buy a bundle of birch branches to whack yourself with and wake up your skin.

People of all ages enjoy relaxing in the heat of a Russian bathhouse.

Musicians perform Russian folk songs accompanied by traditional instruments including the triangular, three-stringed balalaika.

5
THE ARTS

Cultural Treasures

The story of the arts in Russia reaches back to the eighth-century state of Rus. But it is not a story of smooth, steady development. Instead, Russian culture blossomed, then withered under Mongol rule; burst to life under the czars, then struggled to survive under communism. Finally, the end of Soviet rule brought Russia's artists a third awakening with new opportunities and challenges.

Literature

Russia's first written literature appeared in the late ninth century, in biographies of saints penned by Russian Orthodox monks. Early nonreligious writings mixed old legends and folktales with historic records to create imaginative stories about battles and princes.

Not much literature appeared in Russia during the centuries of Mongol rule. But under the czars, renewed contact with Western Europe helped shape Russian poetry, plays, and fables. In Russia's Golden Age of literature, from the 1820s to the 1890s, and Silver Age, from the 1890s to the 1920s, writers

RUSSIA'S LITERARY GIANTS

Alexander Pushkin (1799–1837). Golden Age founder of modern Russian literature. Many Russian children and adults know some of Pushkin's beloved poems and fairy tales by heart.

Fyodor Dostoyevsky (dahs-teh-YEF-skee) (1821–1881). Golden Age master of psychological novels, in which the story takes place partly within the minds of the characters. Dostoyevsky's *The Brothers Karamazov* describes the murder of an evil man by one of his sons.

Count Leo Tolstoy (1828–1910). Great Golden Age novelist whose works examine birth, death, war, love, and duty. Tolstoy's famous novel *War and Peace* brings to life Napoleon's invasion of Russia.

Boris Pasternak (1890–1960). Silver Age poet-novelist awarded the 1958 Nobel Prize in literature for *Doctor Zhivago,* a grand love story set during the Russian Revolution. The government considered Pasternak's novel "anti-Soviet" and forced him to refuse the prize.

Alexander Solzhenitsyn (sol-che-NEET-sen) (1918–   ). Novelist who received the 1970 Nobel Prize in literature for stories based on his seven years in a Soviet prison camp. Solzhenitsyn was forced to leave his homeland for twenty years; he returned after the fall of communism.

blended Western and native Russian influences to create some of literature's greatest masterpieces.

When the Communists took power, writers were ordered to praise the government and describe Soviet life as happy and comfortable. Those who refused were forced to leave the country or were sentenced to long terms in brutal prison camps. Russia's finest writers worked in secret during this period, or wrote and published outside the Soviet Union.

Today Russians are free to write and read whatever they choose. Library shelves at last are filling with long-forbidden works by Russian authors . . . and with paperback mysteries and romances by American authors, too.

Music

For centuries Russian Orthodox priests banned musical instruments from church and called musicians "messengers of the devil." The church's ban delayed the growth of Russian music until the mid-1600s. Then, under the increasing influence of Western Europe, organ music joined the church service. Peasants rediscovered ancient instruments such as the gusli, a ten-string harp, and invented new ones, including the triangular, three-stringed balalaika (ba-leh-LY-keh). The czars set up military bands, court choirs, and orchestras, and wealthy landowners built home theaters for performances of Italian operas.

The music written by Russian composers of this era sounded much like the works of Italian artists. But in 1812, when Russia defeated French emperor Napoleon's invading forces, pride and patriotism swelled the hearts of a new generation of composers. Most famous among them were Modest Mussorgsky, Alexander Borodin, Nikolay Rimsky-Korsakov, and Peter Ilich Tchaikovsky (chy-KAHF-skee), composer of the *1812 Overture* and the *Nutcracker* ballet. In the works of these brilliant artists, a new and distinctly Russian style of music was born. Often based on the legends and history of Russia, their operas, symphonies, and ballets echoed with the rich melodies of native folk songs.

When the Communists took over, composers were told to write only simple, cheerful melodies. Gifted artists, including Igor Stravinsky, Sergey Prokofiev, Dmitry Shostakovich, and Sergey Rachmaninoff, followed their hearts instead, composing masterful works that reflected their dark times. Many

Many styles of music are popular in Russia today including the modern sounds played by these students at Moscow's Institute of Rock and Roll.

Dancers of Russia's world-famous Kirov Ballet company rehearse for a U.S. tour.

talented composers were forced to flee Russia, only to return decades later, after communism's fall.

Today music of all sorts is enjoyed in Russia, from operas and symphonies to jazz and rock and roll. Russian rock groups such as The New Composers and Liuki compete for radio time with popular American performers, including Phil Collins, UB 40, and Queen.

Painting

Nearly all Russian painting before the eighteenth century was religious. Churches glowed from floor to ceiling with colorful wall paintings, mosaics, and special religious paintings called icons. The icons, with their bright, expressive images of biblical characters and events, were considered sacred, and painting them was a holy act.

When Peter the Great brought Western art home to Russia, artists began to paint a greater variety of subjects. Portraits of the wealthy and famous became popular, along with large, dramatic scenes from history, nature, and peasant life.

In the early 1900s artists played with different ways of looking at reality. They created abstract paintings, in which line and color express a mood or idea instead of showing recognizable subjects. But this modern art was banned when the Communists took over, and many fine painters were forced to flee their homeland. Others worked "underground," secretly creating works of art that the public would not see until the 1980s.

Architecture

The style of Russia's churches and many other famous works of architecture was shaped by the Russian Orthodox Church.

The twelfth-century Our Lady of Vladimir, *Russia's most famous icon, is said to have miraculously saved Moscow three times from invading foreign armies.*

The Orthodox faith had its roots in the ancient Byzantine Empire, the eastern part of the old Roman Empire. Many Russian architects adopted the dazzling, multicolored, highly decorative Byzantine style. A distinctive Russian addition to the Byzantine design are the onion-shaped domes that top Russian churches.

Western Europe's influence on Russian architecture shows in many structures built after the seventeenth century, especially in St. Petersburg. Designed by Western artists and architects under the command of Peter the Great, St. Petersburg is filled with churches, fortresses, and mansions built in the grand and elegant Western style called baroque.

The Kremlin in Moscow is a minicity of splendid palaces, churches, towers, and government buildings.

Just outside St. Petersburg, in Petrodvorets, Western Europe's influence shines in the golden statues, fountains, and mansion of Czar Peter's summer palace.

The glittering fountains and mansion of Peter the Great's summer palace, Petrodvorets, near St. Petersburg are spectacular, especially at night.

Information and Entertainment

Newspapers, magazines, radio, television, movies—in the Soviet Union the government controlled all the ways people got information. Most often the information the Soviets spread through these avenues was simply propaganda—lies to glorify the Communist cause. But with the end of Soviet government, a Russian information revolution began.

Today Russia has nearly five thousand independent newspapers, including several hundred in minority languages. There are also several thousand Russian magazines, including a few published just for young readers.

Radio stations in Russia broadcast a variety of news and music programs, including several Western-style mixes of rock music and advertising. On television there are many interesting talk and news programs. One of the hottest shows, *600 Seconds,* is an on-the-scene look at crime and the lives of famous people. *Field of Wonders,* the country's number-one show, is a Russian-language version of *Wheel of Fortune.* TV's number-two spot is held by *Simply Maria,* a soap opera imported from Mexico.

Foreign imports are also popular in Russian movie theaters. *Beverly Hills Cop* and *Back to the Future* were recent megahits, and actors Sylvester Stallone and Arnold Schwarzenegger are top attractions. Russian directors today have a hard time finding money to make new films, but many fine Russian movies that were banned by the Soviets have been released to theaters.

Russia's Treasure Houses

It's no surprise that a country with Russia's rich cultural history has tens of thousands of fine libraries and museums. Princely estates and monasteries and convents (religious retreats for men and for women) now make peaceful settings for priceless collections of native art. Russians spend many free hours in their cities' museums. In difficult times these are perfect places for reflecting on a vast, beautiful country with a rich and unconquerable spirit.

Country Facts

Official Name: Rossiyskaya Federatsiya (Russian Federation)

Capital: Moscow

Location: covers much of eastern Europe and the whole of northern Asia. Northern border is the Arctic Ocean; eastern border, the Pacific Ocean. In the south it touches the Black and Caspian Seas, China, Mongolia, North Korea, and the former Soviet republics of Georgia, Azerbaijan, and Kazakhstan. In the west it borders Norway, Finland, Poland, and the former Soviet republics of Estonia, Latvia, Lithuania, Belarus, and Ukraine.

Area: 6,592,800 square miles (17,075,400 square kilometers). *Greatest distances:* east–west, 6,000 miles (9,650 kilometers); north–south, 2,800 miles (4,500 kilometers)

Elevation: *Highest:* Mount Elbrus, 18,465 feet (5,628 meters), in Caucasus Mountains, southwest Russia. *Lowest:* coast of Caspian Sea, 92 feet (28 meters) below sea level

Climate: long, extremely cold winters and short, hot summers; moderate to light rainfall

Population: 149.6 million. 82 percent Russian; about 120 other ethnic groups. *Distribution:* 74 percent urban, 26 percent rural.

Form of Government: democratic republic.

Important Products: *Natural Resources:* coal, oil, natural gas, iron ore, nickel, copper, silver, gold, and timber. *Agriculture:* grains (wheat, barley, rye, oats), potatoes, and sugar beets. *Industries:* machine tools, tractors, automobiles, electric locomotives, chemicals, and cotton textiles.

Basic Unit of Money: ruble; 1 ruble=100 kopeks

Language: Russian is the official national language. Ethnic groups often speak a native tongue, with Russian as a second language.

Religion: Dominant religion is Russian Orthodox, with about 7,000 churches. Others include Muslim, Roman Catholic, Baptist, Lutheran, Evangelist, and approximately two million Jews.

Flag: Russian Federation flag, adopted in 1991, is the flag used by the Russian Empire from 1699 to 1918. Displays a field of three equal horizontal stripes, with a white bar on top, then blue, then red.

National Anthem: has no title and no words; music is from a 100-year-old opera. A contest is to be held to find words to fit the music.

Major Holidays: New Year's Day, Christmas (January 7), Easter, Women's Day (March 8), Spring Day (May 1), Victory Day (May 9), and Anniversary of the Coup (August 21)

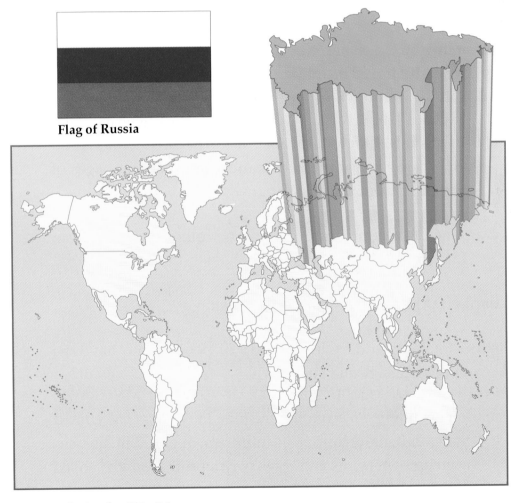

Flag of Russia

Russia in the World

Glossary

autonomous republics: regions within Russia that have their own independent governments and are populated mostly by one of the country's smaller nationality groups

babushka (BAH-boosh-keh): in Russian, "grandmother." The word refers to any elderly Russian woman.

collective farms: large farms set up when the Soviets seized all private farms and combined their lands. Laborers worked on the collective farms and sold their produce back to the government at prices the government set.

communism: a system of government in which a single, all-powerful government party owns and controls all goods and their production

Cyrillic (seh-RI-lik): an alphabet of thirty-three letters, used for writing Russian and a number of other languages of Eastern Europe and Asia

czar: one of the emperors, or supreme rulers, of Russia from 1547 to 1917

dacha (DAH-cheh): a small country cottage

ethnic: having to do with a group of people who have the same language and customs

market economy: an economic system, like that of the United States and many European countries, in which businesses set their own prices and try to earn a profit from the goods and services they provide

Mongols: brutal warriors from eastern Asia who conquered Russia in the thirteenth century A.D. and ruled for 250 years; also called Tatars

plateau: a large, flat land area that is much higher than the land surrounding it. The Central Siberian Plateau, in Siberia, is Russia's largest plateau.

propaganda: false information spread by a government or political party to improve its reputation or position

serfs: peasant farmers who were almost slaves. Serfs were under the control of the landowners and were sold along with the land.

Slavs: members of Europe's largest ethnic group, divided into West Slavs, South Slavs, and East Slavs. Russians are descended from East Slavs who settled in the taiga around the third century A.D.

steppes: flat, grassy, mostly treeless meadows. Russia's fertile steppes begin where the taiga ends.

taiga (TY-ga): an area of forestland, with mostly evergreen trees, that begins just below the tundra

tundra: a flat or gently rolling treeless plain. Russia's tundra is in the far north.

Varangians: Scandinavian warrior-adventurers, related to the Vikings, who conquered Slavic trading centers and established the state of Rus

For Further Reading

Clark, Mary Jane Behrends. *The Commonwealth of Independent States*. Brookfield, Connecticut: The Millbrook Press, 1992.

Flint, David C. *The Former Soviet States: The Russian Federation*. Brookfield, Connecticut: The Millbrook Press, 1992.

Gillies, John. *The New Russia*. New York: Macmillan, Dillon Press, 1994.

Higginbotham, J. *Discovering Russia: People and Places*. New York: State Mutual Book & Periodical Service, 1989.

Kendall, Russ. *Russian Girl: Life in an Old Russian Town*. New York: Scholastic, 1994.

Moscow, Henry, and eds. of *Horizon* Magazine. *Russia Under the Czars*. New York: American Heritage, 1962.

Torchinsky, Oleg. *Russia*, Cultures of the World. New York: Marshall Cavendish, 1994.

World Book Encyclopedia of People and Places. Chicago: World Book, 1993.

Index

Page numbers for illustrations are in boldface

About the Author

"**I**'ve always dreamed of visiting faraway lands, but most of my travels so far have been through the pages of books. This 'journey on paper' to the great nation of Russia has been a wonderful adventure. I hope readers will enjoy sharing the ride!"

Virginia Schomp is an editor and writer whose books for young readers include *The Bottlenose Dolphin* and *The Ancient Greeks.* She lives in Monticello, New York, with her husband, Richard, and their son, Chip.